How to Do Theological Reflection

Thinking, Writing and Living Theologically

Andrew Dunlop

Tutor in Context-based Training and Pioneering

Ridley Hall, Cambrid

GROVE BOOKS LIMITED

RIDLEY HALL RD CAMBRIDGE CB3 9HU

Contents

To the context-based (PC3) students of Ridley Hall and Westcott House.

First Impression September 2022
ISSN 0144-171X
ISBN 978 1 78827 263 6

What is Theological Reflection and Why Do it?

1

The first time many Christians come across the term 'theological reflection' is often when undertaking some form of theological study. Initially it can seem confusing, as people who have been Christians for a long time and are taking their faith seriously often already have a particular way of thinking theologically about life. When something big happens in their lives, such as having to start again in a new place, a change of job or the end of a relationship, they usually try to make sense of it in relation to their faith. They might seek advice from Christian friends, or look for an answer in Scripture, or ask a question such as, 'Where is God in this?' A number of years ago young Christians were being encouraged to ask, 'What would Jesus do?' in each situation they found themselves in.

At its root, theological reflection is simply thinking about an experience and asking questions of faith about it in order to come to a conclusion, perhaps through a conversation with other Christians or formulating thoughts in a journal. In a previous role, when I was pioneering a new church, I did not actively use a formal method of theological reflection, but I did write blog posts and I did talk through issues with trusted friends. On the blog, I would usually describe some thoughts about something I had experienced, ask a faith question that related to it, or bring some Scripture to it, and end with a new way of thinking or some new action I was going to undertake. This is a form of theological reflection.

When theological reflection is taught, our established, intuitive ways of thinking can be challenged by various models for theological reflection. Initially these can seem clunky; difficult to use or inhibiting. However, each model is designed with a particular emphasis and purpose. They might be designed to avoid some usual tendencies that can occur, such as proof-texting from Scripture, or they might be designed to ensure that particular questions are asked about the experience being considered. This booklet will, at its core, describe some of the main methods of theological reflection that are used and taught in theological courses, examine their strengths and weaknesses, and suggest when it might be appropriate to use which model.

Theological Reflection is Theology

When we do theological reflection, we are doing theology.

The former Archbishop of Canterbury Rowan Williams, in addition to his leadership of the Church of England, is respected widely as an academic in the field of the early church fathers and Christian spirituality. He has written books both for an academic and popular audience. Yet when it comes to his theological method—how theology starts—he roots it in experience.

> I assume that the theologian is always beginning in the middle of things. There is a practice of common life and language that is already there, a practice that defines a specific shared way of interpreting human life as lived in relation to God. The meanings of the word 'God' are to be discovered by watching what this community does—not only when it is consciously reflecting in conceptual ways, but it is active, education, or 'inducting,' imagining and worshipping. The theological emerges as a distinct and identifiable figure when these meanings have become entangled with one another, when there is a felt tension between images or practices, when a shape has to be drawn out so that community's practice can be effectively communicated.[1]

According to Williams, theology is found when we reflect upon God in relation to our experiences and religious practice. And when you read Williams, you discover that this reflection also includes a reflection upon Scripture and the great theological writings of the past. But the point that theology emerges from reflection on practice cannot be missed. Many of our most certain doctrines came from a conversation between Scripture and a context or inciting incident. Think of the change in outlook that the two disciples on the Emmaus road underwent. The hope of the resurrection became keenly felt when they had re-evaluated their understanding of Scripture and experienced the risen Christ (Luke 24). Or think of Peter's re-evaluation of God's mission in the light of his rooftop experience (Acts 10)—that the Christian faith was not to be a subset of Judaism, obliged to keep the same purity laws, but that Christ came for all, Jew and Gentile. During the reformation, Martin Luther's understanding of justification by faith alone came as a response to his many years of spiritual despair despite much fasting, penance and confession, and to counter the teaching of the Roman Catholic Church at the time that the buying of indulgences could free the souls of loved ones from purgatory. These Christian doctrines emerged from experiences, which enabled Christians to return to Scripture to develop their thinking, and perhaps see the biblical passages in a new light.

Defining features of Theological Reflection

One of the reasons Christians reflect is to make sense of their life experiences in relation to their faith. It is an 'essential dimension of Christian self-understanding and practice' and is therefore part of Christian discipleship.[2] As we reflect, we may find ourselves challenged in our attitudes or actions. We may find ourselves drawn to change something in our life. Because of this, theological reflection is integrally related to a Christian's walk with God—it is a spiritual exercise which can reveal God's will or presence. As Paul Ballard writes:

> There are no guarantees. There is only the faithful longing and wrestling that can discern, from time to time, God's gracious presence which is so often hidden and obscure.[3]

This point may not be questioned when it is being done intuitively but is easy to miss when reflection models and processes are introduced. Nevertheless, the models and approaches give important structure to a reflection that can enable a deeper engagement with the experience, with theology, with the self, and ultimately with God, when they are treated as a spiritual and not just an academic exercise. In the context of ministry, seeing God through theological reflection can impact the direction of the mission of the church.[4]

Although the precise nature of what theological reflection is has been difficult to define, there is some agreement as to some of the aspects that might go into a theological reflection. Drawing on wider work Sarah Dunlop, Catherine Nancekievill and Pippa Ross-McCabe have identified the following defining features:

- It displays openness to a divine agent: an assumption and dependence on divine participation, an attentiveness to the presence and participation of God.
- It wrestles with Scripture and Christian tradition.
- It connects with an everyday reality, experience, context and/or a specific problem.
- It seeks and assumes transformation of persons and practice—at the very least moving towards naming of some provisional outcomes of the reflection.
- It includes self-awareness and reflexivity, a move beyond reflection which challenges the tendency to see what we expect to see.
- It displays an awareness of complexity, ambiguity and the provisional nature of knowledge.[5]

From these features, I suggest that a good theological reflection should therefore include the following five aspects (though I am not suggesting that they are necessarily taken in this order as a model to be followed). First, there needs to be engagement with an *experience, a context or an issue*. This would include a deep description of what is or was happening with a view to uncovering all the potential issues and perspectives at play.

The second aspect is a detailed engagement with *theology, Scripture* and *Christian tradition*. This should go beyond proof-texting in support of an argument or position. There is no benefit in reflection when one is simply justifying a prior set of beliefs! However, a thoughtful engagement with a biblical text or perspective from theology can challenge previously held assumptions or give a new insight onto a situation.

A third aspect is *reflexivity*, which includes relevant aspects of personal history or experience and engaging with feelings and emotional response to what was happening. For example, should the subject of the reflection be a pastoral incident in which, say, someone at church is verbally bullying another church member, the reflector's reaction to that situation will be quite different if they themselves have been bullied in the past. The situation may trigger all sorts of memories and feelings which will have to be addressed. Reflexivity also includes noting personal positions on issues which may reveal preconceived ideas or biases. For example, as a mixed-race, heterosexual, married man from the UK with a middle-class upbringing, I bring perspectives and experiences that are different from someone who might be, for example, a black, unmarried woman from the US deep south, or a young, white, gay man from Russia. Reflexivity involves noting those positions we bring to a reflection.

Fourth, a reflection might also want to include insights from *non-theological disciplines*, though this is not essential. It may be that insights from psychology or sociology might give a valuable perspective on why something is happening. For example, if reflecting on an incident which includes something relevant to mental health, medical or psychological perspectives on that mental health condition might be pertinent.

All reflections should identify some form of transformation

Finally, all reflections should identify some form of *transformation*. This might be in the form of specific actions to put into practice, or a renewed understanding of self, God or experience which can influence future thinking and action.

Although all theological reflections need the aspects outlined above, the extent to which each aspect is addressed might depend on the nature of the reflection at hand. For example, I once wrote a reflection on the extent of social isolation found on new-build housing developments and how the church might respond, a question that had arisen from my previous ministry experience. Whilst some reflexivity was important in this reflection (such as the nature of my involvement and my understanding of what the church is for), this was not the focus of the reflection. I did, however, engage in depth with the theology of the social trinity and with a sociological perspective on social capital. Another reflection, written by practical theologian Heather Walton, takes a journaling style (which will be explored in the next chapter) and is extremely reflexive, although light on formal theology.[6] The purpose of the reflection affects the model or approach we may choose as well as the degree to which each of the aspects mentioned above are addressed.

If We Do it Already, Why Do We Need Models?

As I have already mentioned, Christians usually do some form of theological reflection intuitively. They might write a journal, talk and pray through issues with other Christians, or take time out on their own to think through an issue and talk to God. But if this if the case, why do we need models of theological reflection, and why are there so many?

Recent research by Dunlop, Nancekievill and Ross-McCabe attempted to identify how Christians engaged in theological reflective practice.[7] Participants in the study, who were all lay Anglicans (*ie* those who were not ordained and had formal theological training), were asked to talk about two things: how they had processed a significant incident in their life, and any other event that had occurred during the previous week. Whilst such reflection had potential to be a theologically and spiritually enriching task, in practice it was generally underdeveloped. Participants demonstrated a willingness to engage with God, but engagement with the Bible, theology or Christian tradition was only rarely mentioned, and even then, not in particular depth. Whilst most participants described a transformation—a change in their practice or understanding—after doing the reflection, many were unable to engage reflexively with the task, and were particularly hesitant to process negative emotions. A final finding of the study indicated a reluctance to allow the process to challenge their pre-existing knowledge. In summary, whilst the reflections were deemed valuable, the authors concluded that church leaders might find ways of encouraging and equipping Christians to wrestle with experiences together in order to 'enable a deepening dialogue with [our] generous God.'[8]

Church leaders might find ways of equipping Christians to wrestle with experiences together

The advantage of using particular models or methods in theological reflection is to encourage such depth. With a careful choice of model suited to the experience—the subject of the reflection—important aspects of theological reflection such as biblical or theological engagement, or reflexivity, are less likely to be forgotten.

There are disadvantages as well, of course. Some students can struggle when they encounter theological reflection models for the first time. They feel that a task that previously had come quite naturally can become stymied or limited by the process. This does not have to be the case. Familiarity with the models or approaches can bring freedom. In a way, it might be a bit like learning to drive or learning a new sport. At the beginning the new driver has to concentrate quite hard on controlling the vehicle, thinking about the different controls and pedals. But after a while the controls become second nature to the driver and they can simply concentrate on getting safely to their destination. Similarly, a professional footballer might spend hours practising simple passes or ball control skills, so that, when they are playing a match, these skills come naturally and can be improvised in the heat of the moment. With theological reflection, as the models become familiar, reflective practitioners might want to leave some of the specifics of them behind, knowing they can go with the flow of reflecting without neglecting important aspects.

In the next chapter I will introduce some of the commonly taught models and approaches, outlining their strengths and weaknesses and suggesting what sort of reflections they are best suited to.

Methods, Models or Approaches to Theological Reflection

2

A number of methods, models, approaches and processes have been suggested for theological reflection,[9] and they have been categorized in a variety of ways.[10] I am going to divide them into three broad groups for the sake of simplicity, though other categorizations exist. These reflection models are based on cycles, and emphasize reflexivity and conversational approaches.

Reflection Cycles

The most commonly taught models for theological reflection are based on what has come to be known as the pastoral cycle.[11] This four-stage cycle is easy to remember and, beginning with a deep description of the experience, takes the reflector sequentially through stages of exploration of the situation, theological reflection on that exploration and renewed action (see Fig 1).

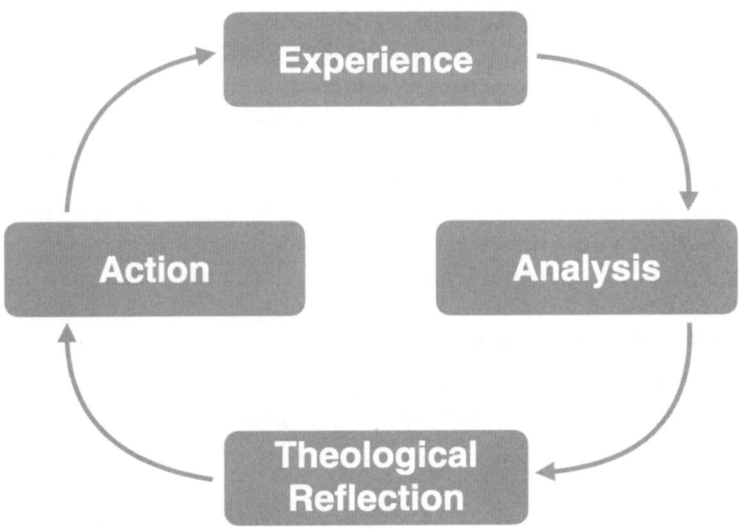

Fig 1: The Pastoral Cycle

Richard Osmer helpfully summarized a similar approach by asking four questions. Although he expresses them as four tasks, rather than in a cycle, and states that they often spiral back to one another, he tends to present them sequentially.[12]

- *What is going on?* This is what Osmer calls the descriptive-empirical task. It is an information gathering exercise which allows the reflector to see patterns and dynamics in the situation.
- *Why is it going on?* This is the interpretative task which attempts to understand why such patterns and dynamics exist, perhaps drawing on non-theological sources to do so.
- *What ought to be going on?* In this normative task, theological and biblical sources are used to interpret the situation and to guide practice.
- *How might we respond?* This task—the pragmatic task—draws together the learning from the other tasks to determine strategies for action.

These processes tend to operate in one direction, with the description of experience leading to an analysis of it, followed by bringing theology to it (in the form of biblical insight, formal theology or learning from the Christian tradition), and resulting in renewed action or learning. This process gives theology a normative or correcting influence over the process. It also gives theology the final say, over and above insights from any other disciplines that may have been discussed. Depending on your perspective of what theology is and how it should relate to other forms of knowledge, you may not find this to be an issue.[13] However, there are occasions where our theological analysis can challenge our non-theological assumptions *and* where non-theological analysis (*ie* insights from non-theological sources of knowledge) might challenge our theological assumptions.

In order to account for this, Emanuel Lartey introduced a variation of the pastoral cycle which is a little more flexible and allows for different insights to challenge one another (see Fig 2).[14] After the description of the experience comes the *situational analysis,* which brings perspectives from non-theological disciplines to the experience. The third stage is the *theological analysis* which is allowed to question the encounter as well as challenge insights from the situational analysis. A fourth stage, the *situational analysis of theology,* enables the insights from the theological analysis to be questioned both by the experience and by the outcomes of the second stage. Finally, the reflector moves to explore an appropriate response. The key difference to the pastoral cycle is the addition of this extra stage ensuring that theology and other insights get to question one another, illustrated by the use of multi-directional arrows in the diagram.

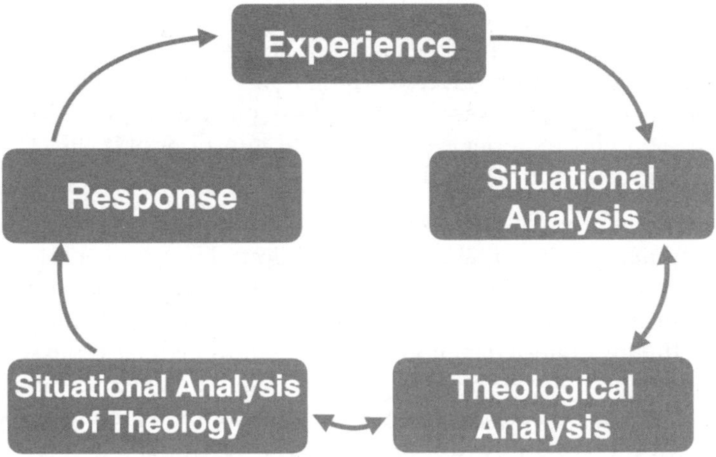

Fig 2: Lartey's Pastoral Cycle

In all these cycles, after reaching a point of response, the reflector is brought to a new place of action or understanding. Often new questions arise, or the reflector may want to try out a new action before reflecting upon it again. Because of this, Laurie Green rightly identifies that the reflector is brought to a new place, hence the processes are not cyclical, but form more of a spiral (see Fig 3).[15] Therefore, reflectors may want to go through the process more than once in order to get to the heart of the matter.

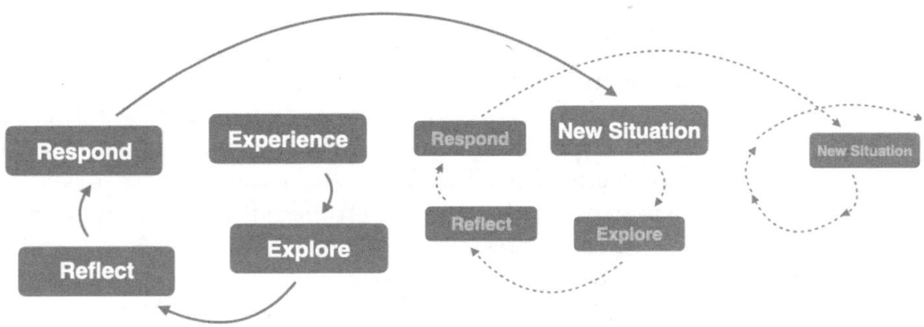

Fig 3: Green's 'Doing Theology' Spiral

Advantages and Drawbacks

Cycles such as these are generally quite clear and easy to follow, but they are not suitable for reflections on all situations. They are helpful because of their simplicity, clear process and flexibility, and offer an easy way into formal theological reflection. Because there are particular points in the cycle where theological engagement is expected, they can ensure that this important aspect of a reflection is not neglected. There is also space for insight from other disciplines, and the processes clearly lead to a place of response. Because they start from a point of experience and ask clear questions of it, they can be good for reflecting upon critical incidents.

However, there are some drawbacks with the cycle approach, and methods of this kind may not be suitable for all situations. First, for complex scenarios where there is a great variety of different voices, the process may not help the reflector to draw out all the nuances of the situation. In these, other approaches (below) may bear more fruit. Secondly, whilst reflexivity can be spread throughout the whole reflection, as it is not named specifically in the cycles, it is easy for aspects such as personal positions or feelings to be missed. Thirdly, reflection cycles such as these have been critiqued because they have the potential to limit theology, and perhaps even the Christian faith itself, to just one part of the reflection cycle.[16] This can be an issue but, if the whole process is undertaken in the context of prayer and perhaps even a living Christian community, it can be argued that the whole process *is* theological as it is seeking to understand the mind of God.[17] However, there are other approaches to theological reflection that more overtly provide a space for a faith position, biblical insight or Christian theology throughout the process.

Models that Emphasize Reflexivity

Some degree of reflexivity should be a part of all theological reflections. As noted above, the reflector brings certain preconceived notions and assumptions to the reflection, and in some cases there may be a particular personal aspect to the subject matter. It is always good to acknowledge these, and in some cases these pre-existing positions or personal aspects may be challenged. If reflecting on a situation that involves a personal dimension or a particular emotional reaction, it is important to ensure that reflexivity is attended to. Although all reflection cycles, models and approaches allow space for reflexivity, some are particularly suited, bringing out the positions, emotions and issues involved. I will highlight three.

Jane Leach's Pastoral Theology as Attention

Jane Leach's model of 'pastoral theology as attention' helps the reflector identify all the different voices that may be contributing to a situation, including the 'voice' of their own position.[18] It is particularly suited to reflecting on situations of conflict, where there may be lots of different opinions in the mix. It is framed around five questions, with sub-questions.

- *Attention to the voices*. This first question draws the reflection to consider all the voices involved in the situation or conflict. What are they saying? What feelings are being expressed? Whose voices are absent or being silenced? Whose voices are being mediated by someone else? These last two sub-questions enable the voices of the oppressed, marginalized or simply the shy to be considered, although in the case of silent or mediated voices, a reflection after the fact may never be able fully to understand sentiments that have never been articulated.
- *Attention to the wider issues*. The reflector is invited to consider trends in the culture of the organization, of wider society, and the type of human behaviour being exhibited. How might the past have shaped the present? Are there insights from other academic disciplines or witnesses from the context that might help us understand the culture better?
- *Attention to my own voice*. This is the question which specifically calls for reflexivity. As the reflector, what is my role in the situation? How do I (or did I) feel at the time? Where do I locate myself in relation to the issues being discussed so far in the reflection? What are my instincts about the heart of the issue in this situation and where do these instincts come from?
- *Attention to the theological tradition*. Here, the voices of theology are heard. Are there implicit ethical values being practised in this situation? Are there biblical texts that resonate or challenge what is going on? If so, why these and not others? What has my church tradition said about the issues identified? What other theological resources can be brought to bear? These could be insights from theologians, liturgy, church texts, hymns or practices of the church.
- *Attention to the mission of the church*. Given the discussion that will have emerged from the previous questions, how might the reflection be brought to a response in relation to the mission of the particular church, or wider church, and what might the reflector's own role be in that? Depending on the subject of the reflection, the response may be either an action to undertake or a renewed sense of understanding which can contribute to ministry in that context.

Leach's approach is an excellent one for identifying the core issues and multiple perspectives in complex situations, particularly those of conflict. It can help identify the power structures at play and, particularly, who may be being marginalized or silenced. The specific questions attending to the reflector's own voice allow their own positions and emotional responses to be considered. The dedicated attention to theology ensures that the voices from Scripture, tradition and Christian experience are not overlooked. In my experience, this has been a very popular model with students.

Care has to be taken with this model, however, particularly if you are using it in a group or writing a reflection for others to read. Whilst the naming of the voices is an important and vital part of the approach, because it broadens the scope of the reflection to include so many perspectives, those reflecting sometimes either spend too much time or space on this question and end up neglecting or skimming over other important aspects such as theology, or they struggle to bring the reflection back to focus in on the core issue. It is important, after identifying the issues, to choose which aspects of theology and culture to engage with in depth in order to bring the reflective process to a place of response. Jane Leach originally developed this approach whilst working with trainee Methodist ministers in South Africa reflecting on visits with healthcare professionals in South Africa as they sought to develop an appropriate response for their churches to HIV/AIDS in the area. The five questions Leach left with the group could be used over a period of time as they continued to reflect on the situation together.[19] If being used as part of a reflective practice group, this model may therefore be best employed over the course of several sessions. If reflecting alone, the reflector may want to come back to different stages in the approach over the course of time.

Theological reflection is not a simplifying process but one of complexification

Leach's model has the tendency to broaden the scope of the situation, highlighting many different influences upon it. Whilst this can be disconcerting at first, sometimes seeming like the factors relating to an issue are growing out of control, complexification is actually a strength of theological reflection (and should feature in all reflections, regardless of the approach used). Complexity helps us understand all the factors at play, in order to come to a more informed and nuanced response. Theological reflection is not a simplifying process which yields a simple response, but a process of complexification drawn from many sources.[20] This complexification is often an initial stumbling block for those undertaking theological reflection; however, once it is understood that theological reflection complexifies rather than simplifies, reflectors become more able to reject simplistic solutions, to allow their theology and initial perceptions to develop, and to live with theological ambiguity in their ministry.[21]

Movement Into Insight

Presented in a book called *The Art of Theological Reflection,* Patricia O'Connell Killen and John de Beer's method invites the reflector to begin their reflection by attending to their feelings (see Fig 4).[22] As in many other models, they are invited, first, to enter into the experience under consideration through a deep, concrete and accurate description. At this point, the reflector is to avoid making judgments or providing analysis. Instead of an intellectual analysis that might, in some cases, remain on a detached conceptual level, the reflector is then invited to pay attention to the feelings that arise within them when recalling the situation. Were they feeling uncomfortable, distraught or confused? Was there an instinctive gut reaction that was difficult to put words to? Some experiences result in those experiencing them feeling physically sick, having a heightened sense of anxiety, or a giddy sense of elation. These feelings are to be noted and named.

From here, the reflector is invited to conjure up an image or metaphor which could describe this feeling. Sometimes images can more accurately depict complex feelings than words. For example, the feeling could be like carrying the burden of a steel rod on your shoulders, being locked out of a party in your own house, or the feeling of joy and satisfaction that comes when standing on a mountain top after completing a particularly difficult ascent. The image can either be described or created. One of my students who was a particularly gifted artist reflected on the self-giving of two female priests during the pandemic and created a beautiful pencil drawing of the Virgin Mary in reaction to how women have been treated by the church throughout history. This was no Mary as traditionally depicted by Renaissance painters. His Mary was youthful but strong, dignified and defiant, unhaloed and earthy. She is represented as a willing co-agent in God's salvation plan, 'working autonomously with God at great personal risk.'[23]

In a stage Killen and de Beer call 'insight,' the image, which represents the outworking of feelings or emotions encountered during the experience, is then interrogated as it is drawn into conversation with theological tradition. The authors suggest four aspects of theory to draw upon: tradition (which includes Scripture, theology and doctrine as well as the history of the church); culture (of the society, group, place, cultural artefacts); action (the previous experience or lived narrative of the reflector); and positions (what we bring to the reflection in terms of our understandings, assumptions, or theological biases). Each of these four aspects challenges and informs one another in relation to the image. In the example above, the student allowed the image to challenge cultural understandings of women including how women's priestly ministry has been understood (or rejected) throughout history, whilst at the same time being informed by theological understandings of Mary alongside biblical texts.

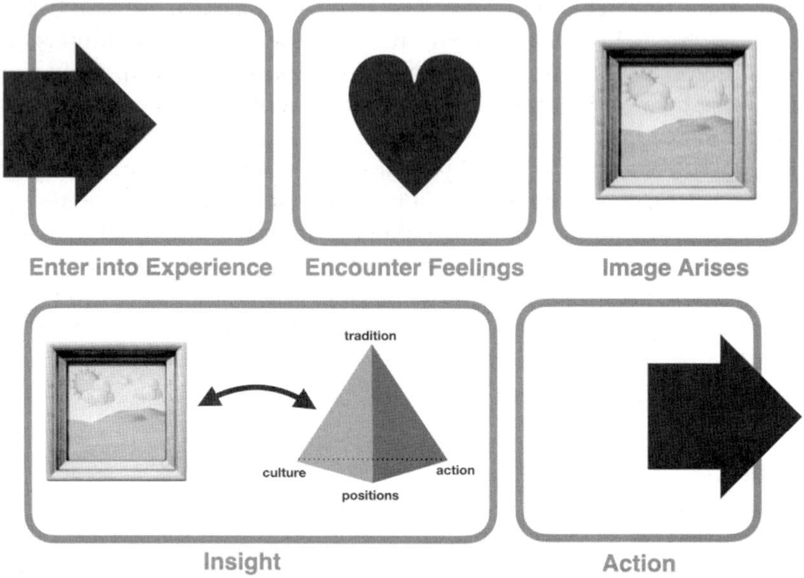

Fig 4: Killen and De Beer's 'Movement into Insight'

This conversation leads to, in Killen and de Beer's final section, a call for renewed action or insight. The student identified two insights that emerged from his reflection on Mary. The first articulated a challenge to a worldview that often values women on their outward appearance—an insight that is by no means unique to that reflection. In the second, he suggested that the experience of Mary willingly giving her body as a vessel for the Son arguably makes women *more* suitable for priestly ministry than men. Many may want to push back on that insight; however, my point here is to illustrate the strength that such an image-based approach to theological reflection can bring.

Killen and de Beer's model, like others, is not suitable for every reflective scenario. However, for the right situation, it has two important advantages over other models. First, it is highly reflexive and forces the participants to take account of their emotions, recognizing them as important sources of insight. Secondly, by introducing images, the cognitive part of the brain (that is, the part that often wants us to rush towards an answer as our initial response) is put to one side in the first instance, enabling other important sources of insight to be brought to the reflection.

Writing as Reflexive Practice

Of course, as I mentioned earlier, theological reflection happens most naturally either through a conversation with trusted Christian friends or through writing in a journal or blog. In *Writing Methods in Theological Reflection*, practical theologian Heather Walton proposes three different writing styles to theological reflection, with slightly different nuances depending on the aims of the reflection.[24] She illustrates each with engaging examples. Her first approach, autoethnography (in essence, the study of the self), involves telling evocative stories which deepen or expand the theme from the reflector's life that is the subject of the reflection. Her second writing method, journaling, is perhaps the most familiar and easiest to grasp. Journals can relate to a critical incident and its aftermath, spiritual growth over a season, or learning on an issue over a period of time. She gives examples of a learning journal as she thinks through how to teach a new class on creative writing and theology, and a spiritual journal in which she charts her journey from anxiousness to peace during a dark time in her life. Finally, she describes life writing. In thinking about the journey that has led to a particular stage in life, the subject is able to construct a story that helps them discover more about themselves and about God. An example of this would be drawing out and discussing a call to ministry that may have evolved over several years. Walton argues that *Confessions* by the early church father, Augustine of Hippo, is perhaps the earliest example of this type of writing.

There are several advantages to these types of approaches. First, they are highly reflexive. The subject of such reflections is usually the self or the reactions of the self to a particular incident. Because of this they can be particularly useful if trying to work through something. Secondly, these approaches seem quite natural and intuitive. Journaling, for example, involves writing and thinking each day, much like keeping a diary. Thirdly, writing like this can help direct a reflector away from linear arguments, enabling an issue to be broadened, deepened and complexified. However, because of the lack of structure, it is easy for some of the essential aspects of theological reflections mentioned in the first chapter to be overlooked. Most likely to be overlooked is a detailed theological analysis. For example, in 2003 Walton published a personal and reflexive account of her journey through IVF fertility treatment.[25] It is a highly engaging read as she grapples with the emotions of that period in her life whilst juggling her work and ministry. However, speaking as one half of a couple that has also been through the infertility rollercoaster, there is a lack of serious theological or biblical engagement with relevant texts in this article. Could the experiences of barren women in the Old Testament—Sarah (Genesis 18) or Hannah (1 Samuel 1)—or the promises made to Israel through Isaiah that the 'barren' women will 'burst into song' (Isa 54.1) add insight to the reflection? The examples Walton gives in *Writing Methods* do tend to contain more theology than her IVF example. Nevertheless, Walton's approaches can be valuable for theological reflections that require a reflexive emphasis so long as they are taken alongside an intention to ensure that theological engagement is not lacking in the reflection.

Conversational Approaches: Four Voices and Four Sources

There are two other approaches to theological reflection that I will highlight here, which are simple to comprehend but bring out complexity and theological depth. Both aim to put different sources of theology and experience into conversation with one another. Again, I will emphasize here that, as with reflexivity, all approaches to theological reflection should have a degree of theological conversation between the sources or stages of the reflection. These approaches simply emphasize this point in the way they are conceived.

The first approach is valuable because of its theological depth. The 'four voices of theology' were not originally developed for theological reflection, but as part of a theological participative empirical research approach called Theological Action Research.[26] However, the four voices began to be used outside of their Theological Action Research framework as an analytical tool for theological reflection, and as such it is worth exploring how they may best be used. They aim to highlight different theological sources that might be operating in a given situation. The voices are:

- *Operant*: theology embedded in the practices of the situation or of a group.
- *Espoused*: theology articulated by participants of such practices.
- *Normative*: theology from sources that the group name as authoritative.
- *Formal*: theology from academia, tradition, or biblical sources.[27]

These voices are not discrete; there can be some overlap. One of the advantages of this approach is that it ensures that theology from practices and beliefs is taken seriously and put into conversation with normative and formal sources of theology. There can be a danger in some models of theological reflection that normative and formal theology is used as a trump card, a correcting influence on practice. Indeed, in Osmer's method, the normative is described as a task alongside the question 'What ought to be going on?' implying that it has some priority over other tasks.[28] As part of the four voices, the normative is a voice alongside the other theological voices.

The four voices approach has the benefit of highlighting important theologies that may be missed whilst also recognizing complexity in the situation. For example, if reflecting on an experience of worship that is proposed to be changed, the operant theology of, say, the rituals and practices that take place or the layout of chairs or pews needs to be discussed alongside any normative theology that might be leading to the proposals for change. Sometimes operant theologies reveal important issues that might have been previously unarticulated.

In group theological reflection, this approach works best when the group is reflecting on a shared experience, so all can help identify the different voices at play. If the experience is brought by only one person in a group but not shared by the others, this can have the effect of making the experience-bringer a gatekeeper for all the theological voices. It is also important not to jump straight to identifying the voices: the voices are the mechanics of the conversation, not the structure. Using open questions to draw out the discussion before formally identifying the voices can help avoid treating them too discretely from the beginning, and therefore help to identify the overlaps and challenges between them. At the end of the discussion, learning or action points should be identified.[29]

For written theological reflections, similar points apply, although it is likely that another approach for the reflection may be more suitable. Nevertheless, the reflector should acknowledge their role in identifying and interpreting all the theological voices. Their preconceived positions will take a larger role in forming the interpretative lens through which all the voices are seen. Once again, as the four voices were not originally developed as a method for theological reflection, it will be important to identify the learning or response after the voices have been identified and discussed.

The second conversational approach to theological reflection is valuable because of its flexibility and simplicity. Drawing on one section from Killen and de Beer's model, O'Neill and Shercliff picture theological reflection as a conversation between four sources, in an approach which includes all the essential aspects of reflection mentioned in chapter one.[30] The sources are:

- *Tradition*—which includes theology, the Bible and traditions of the church.
- *Culture*—including societal trends and insights from non-theological disciplines.
- *Experience*—an issue, problem, scenario or theme. (This source has been changed from 'action' in Killen and de Beer's approach.)

- *Position*—which would include your current assumptions, biases, as well as emotions.

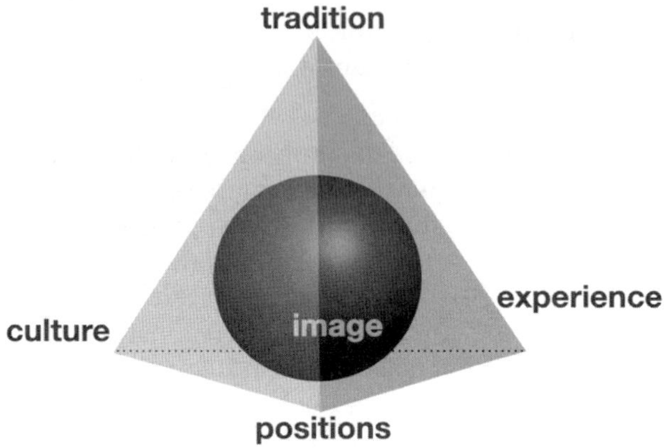

Fig 5: The Four Sources approach

O'Neill and Shercliff do not propose a method (that is, a structured process) for the reflection—one can start with any of the four sources. The only stipulation is that the reflection is a conversation, written or verbal, between all four. An image can still be generated (but is not essential to the approach), in which case it is through the image that each of the four sources travels in conversation with one another (see Fig 5). For example, in the context of a Bible study, a passage might be shared first. A member of the group may then share a personal experience that has been brought to mind which the rest of the group wants to reflect on. From there, the group might want to place the experience and the passage from Scripture into conversation with further theology or Bible passages, cultural trends and previously held belief. In this example, the four-source model is being used, but experience has not been the launching point. Alternatively, it may be that a conversation has arisen regarding a particular social trend which gives rise to some feelings and an image coming to mind. Only from this starting point is experience or theological context brought to the discussion. So O'Neill and Shercliff's approach is flexible and conversational.

This leads nicely onto the questions framing the next chapter. Most theological reflection processes tend to start with experience first, but does it matter where one starts? Do the models, in and of themselves, carry any theological assumptions?

Starting Points for Theological Reflection: Does it Matter?

3

The question of whether starting points matter is actually a question of where the weight of authority lies in a theological conversation. Ultimately this comes down to the theological position of the reflector. To simplify (and perhaps stereotype) the positions, do we interpret Scripture or doctrine in the light of experience or interpret experience in the light of Scripture or doctrine? I am not going to suggest an answer to this, although I have my preference; each must come to their own conclusion and, in reality, our positions likely sit on a spectrum rather than this being a binary choice. It is, however, important to note that all positions require an interpretation of Scripture.

In many theological reflection models, the starting point is experience. This makes sense, as we often come to theological reflection with a particular experience in mind. However, I do not believe that the starting point of experience automatically skews the theology in one direction or another. In his instructional textbook *Introducing Practical Theology*, Pete Ward argues for a gospel-based practical theology.[31] Putting aside divisions of interpretation which might be characterized as liberal or conservative, Ward asserts that the source of truth is in fact the person of Jesus Christ, therefore both Scripture/doctrine and experience need to be held together in pursuit of him. 'Doctrine, then, is always relative to the rich and deep complexity that is the Word.'[32] And of course, the Word is a person. Therefore, much more important than the starting point is the theology that is brought to the experience during the reflection, how it is handled, and whether they together lead the reflector towards a transformation in Christ.

In many theological reflection models, the starting point is experience

Nevertheless, because the starting point is experience, some, such as Helen Collins, have argued that this undermines the neutrality of a method. For example, it is often cited that the development of the pastoral cycle comes through the liberation thinking and educational theories of David Kolb or Paolo Freire.[33] Their aim was to take the realities of oppression and injustice seriously and to enable empowerment, justice, action and participation. But because they privilege experience, Collins argues, pastoral-cycle based approaches are human-centred rather than God-centred. Furthermore, they emphasize the experience of the present over both the experience of the past and eschatological concerns. The results, she argues, are that these 'experience first' cycles disadvantage the Bible, often lumping it in with Christian tradition and doctrine, and interpreting it in the light of experience. The implication is that her preferred understanding of interpreting life's experience in the light of faith and Scripture has been flipped on its head.

To be clear, I do not believe that starting with experience necessarily has to result in a diminishing of Scripture; it all depends on how Scripture, doctrine and Christian tradition are handled within the reflection. Nevertheless, Collins proposes a model which starts with Scripture, and which she claims can be useful for personal or group reflection as well as for use within church leadership groups or PCCs.[34]

The model has four stages all framed around the understanding that the participants are encountering God in each. It begins with reading and meditating on a passage from *Scripture*. This could be taken from the day's Lectionary reading or a Bible reading plan, or could have been selected for another purpose. Participants may undertake *Lectio Divina*, slowly allowing the passages of Scripture to be deeply heard. The group asks questions such as, 'What does this passage tell us about God or ourselves?' or, 'What might the Holy Spirit be saying in this passage?' From the discussion, a theme may emerge. After a time of silence, allowing the discussion of the passage or theme to settle in participants' minds, the group shares *testimony*—stories of what the passage might be raising in their minds. For example, a theme of exile may have emerged from a study of Jeremiah 29, which may lead participants to share times when they felt excluded, alone or exiled from the place they feel they belong. After choosing just one of these situations to focus on, the group *discerns* how this experience complexifies their understanding of the passage. Insights from other disciplines, experiences or traditions may be brought into the conversation at this point. It is worth noting that the primacy of Scripture is preserved here, as these insights serve to complexify the understanding of Scripture, rather than Scripture being brought in at a later point after insights from these perspectives have already been discussed. Finally, participants are invited to reflect on their *encounter* with God throughout the process and reflect on how they are being called to *participate* in God's kingdom and mission in the light of the discussion.

These insights serve to complexify the understanding of Scripture

The strength of this method is that Collins is squarely locating theological reflection within the life of faith. They are not methods to be applied like skills, arbitrarily to an incident or experience with the aim of finding a pragmatic solution to a problem, but they flow from the faith life of the participant and therefore by extension, from engagement with God through his Spirit. Traditional Christian spiritual disciplines, such as reading the Bible, praying, worshipping, participating in the eucharist, meditating, or being in silence or solitude are all seen to be sources of theology useful to such reflection, as they flow from the dynamic life of faith in God. They could even be considered as starting points for reflection. However, it has to be stated that most often, people come to theological reflection with a specific experience in mind which may have flowed from one of these spiritual experiences or have come from somewhere else. Whilst Collins does not discount her method in such circumstances, in these cases other models may be more intuitive.[35]

Collins is by no means the only proponent of a model that does not start with experience. Gary O'Neill and Liz Shercliff's *four sources* approach and the *four voices* approach, both outlined above, could technically begin with any of the four stages. Likewise, a journaling approach has the freedom to place any source first in the writing. But what Collins' method has done is to highlight helpfully how the different elements are handled within a model. I do not believe that this means that particular models are more conservative, liberal or whatever, but rather are influenced by the theology brought to the reflection. Indeed, I have read an excellent example from a student using Collins' model, starting with Scripture, which engaged with psychology, gender-critical studies and trauma theology. But regardless of the model we may be using, we will want to think about how we are handling Scripture, tradition, experience and other disciplines, and how we allow their insights to influence, critique or even override one another.

4 Summary

This booklet has outlined some of the main methods, approaches and models that can be used in theological reflection. Whether you are coming to theological reflection through theological study or simply to engage more deeply with God in your own faith life, I hope it has outlined some of the main arguments and issues. Fundamentally, though, theological reflection is about engaging with God, and whilst it can be as simple as sitting and thinking or praying alone or chatting through an issue with a Christian friend, the kind of models outlined in this booklet can help add more depth and structure to our thinking and praying.

The key in all of them, as we spend time with God working through an issue, is that we are willing to change. Reflection helps us understand something deeper or in a new way, as we open ourselves up to the guidance of the Holy Spirit. It should lead us into a transformation into the way of Christ, in whatever situation we are reflecting upon. Therefore, we need to be open to new ideas, and to weigh them up in the light of Scripture, theology, experience, tradition or insights from any other disciplines. Consequently, your position matters. Because we bring certain preferences, biases and beliefs into the reflection, these will inevitably affect the direction the reflection takes. Having a pre-existing position is not a bad thing, but identifying what these positions may be might open us up to gently challenging them, leading to a richer and deeper reflective process.

It is vital that we take time to attend to the learning from the reflective process

It is also vital that we take time at the end of the process to attend to the learning from the reflective process, whether we are writing for an academic audience, reflecting in a personal capacity only, or leading a group in a reflection. This stage enables us to draw out the points of transformation, changed action or renewed understanding at the end of the reflection. It ultimately embeds the outcomes of the discussion in our practice.

As this booklet has outlined, different models have particular strengths, and can help open up our reflective process in a variety of ways. Being acquainted with a range of different reflective models gives us greater variety and enables us to select the model most suited to the experience or subject we are reflecting upon.

Finally, may I encourage you to engage in reflection not only in a personal capacity. Theological reflection can be useful in one-to-one supervision such as between a vicar and curate, line manager and youth worker, or mentor and mentee. Reflection can help groups such as church leadership teams, PCCs or peer support groups grapple with an issue and / or discern the way forward in mission. It is by no means necessary that all members of the group understand all the different models in order for reflection to be valid. But a facilitator who understands the aspects at play can sensitively guide a group through the reflective process to come to a renewed understanding or common way forward for the issue at hand. Ultimately, all such reflection is vital for continued growth in ministry, and I hope some of the approaches outlined here can be helpful to your ministry as you discern how God may be speaking in your context.

Notes

1 R Williams, *On Christian Theology*, Challenges in Contemporary Theology (Oxford: Blackwell, 2000) p xii.

2 P Ballard, 'Theological Reflection and Providence,' *Practical Theology*, 1.3 (2008), 285–289 (p 286).

3 *ibid*, p 288.

4 Pete Ward talks about reflection making 'a difference to the ongoing life of the church' in *Introducing Practical Theology: Mission, Ministry, and the Life of the Church* (Grand Rapids, MI: Baker Academic, 2017) p 96.

5 S Dunlop, C Nancekievill and P Ross-McCabe, 'Exploring the Reflective Practice of Anglican Laity: Finding Manna in the Desert,' *Practical Theology*, 14.4 (2021), 309–322 (p 312).

6 H Walton, 'Advent: Theological Reflections on IVF,' *Theology & Sexuality*, 9.2 (2003), 201–209.

7 Dunlop, Nancekievill and Ross-McCabe, *op cit*.

8 Dunlop, Nancekievill and Ross-McCabe, *op cit*, p 320.

9 Practical theologians use a variety of language to describe what is going on in theological reflection. They can be called methods, models, approaches or processes. Whitehead and Whitehead distinguish between a model, indicating the sources that are used in a reflection, and a method detailing the steps or stages (J D Whitehead and E Eaton Whitehead, *Method in Ministry: Theological Reflection and Christian Ministry* (Lanham, MD: Rowman and Littlefield, 1995) pp 3–17). For a helpful analysis of the language used see H Collins, *Reordering Theological Reflection: Starting with Scripture* (London: SCM Press, 2020) pp 10–11.

10 For example Pete Ward separates them into two broad categories: those that follow the pastoral cycle and those that do not, although he indicates several sub-categories in the second category (Ward, *op cit*, pp 95–114). Thompson *et al* note six categories to theological reflection approaches which include cyclical processes, variations on cyclical processes, reflections on first-person verbatim accounts, using imagination, narrative reflection, and other methods. J Thompson, S Pattison and R Thompson, *SCM Studyguide to Theological Reflection* (London: SCM Press, 2019) pp 50–71.

11 See P H Ballard and J Pritchard, *Practical Theology in Action: Christian Thinking in the Service of Church and Society* (London: SPCK, 2006) pp 81–95.

12 R R Osmer, *Practical Theology: An Introduction* (Grand Rapids, MI: William B Eerdmans, 2008) pp 4–12.

13 The nature of how theology relates to other disciplines is called correlation and has been discussed at length elsewhere. For a suitable short introduction to the issue, see Ward, *op cit*, pp 77–86.

14 See E Lartey, 'Practical Theology as a Theological Form,' *Contact*, 119.1 (1996), pp 21–25.

15 L Green, *Let's Do Theology: Resources for Contextual Theology* (London: Mowbray, 2009) pp 19–27.

16 Ward, *op cit*, pp 50–51.

17 C Watkins, *Disclosing Church: An Ecclesiology Learned from Conversations in Practice* (London: Routledge, 2020) p 44.

18 J Leach, 'Pastoral Theology as Attention,' *Contact*, 153.1 (2007), 19–32.

19 Leach, *op cit*, pp 21–22.

20 See K Turpin, 'The Complexity of Local Knowledge,' in J-A Mercer and B Miller-McLemore (eds), *Conundrums in Practical Theology* (Boston, MA: Brill, 2016) pp 250–275.

21 Quentin Chandler undertook empirical research with those learning formal theological reflection approaches for the first time. He found that complexification was one of five 'threshold concepts,' vital to development of theological reflection skills. Such a concept is one that might be difficult to grasp initially but once understood opens the door to deeper knowledge. See Q Chandler, 'Conversations beyond the Threshold: An Exploration of Theological Reflection among Lay Ministry Students' (unpublished doctoral thesis, Anglia Ruskin University, 2015) pp 98–101, available at: https://arro.anglia.ac.uk/id/eprint/700185 (accessed 29 June 2020); Q Chandler, 'Cognition or Spiritual Disposition? Thresho ld Concepts in Theological Reflection,' *Journal of Adult Theological Education*, 13.2 (2016), 90–102 (pp 96–97).

22 P O'Connell Killen and J De Beer, *The Art of Theological Reflection* (New York: Crossroad, 1994) pp 20–45.

23 This example is used with permission of the student.

24 H Walton, *Writing Methods in Theological Reflection* (London: SCM Press, 2014).

25 H Walton, 'Advent,' *Theology and Sexuality*, 9(1) (2003), pp 201–209.

26 For an introduction to Theological Action Research see the founding team's initial work: H Cameron *et al*, *Talking about God in Practice: Theological Action Research and Practical Theology* (London: SCM Press, 2010). One member of the team, Clare Watkins, offers more in-depth analysis, including findings from their own projects using the method in *Disclosing Church: An Ecclesiology Learned from Conversations in Practice* (London: Routledge, 2020).

27 Cameron *et al, op cit*, pp 53–56.

28 Osmer, *op cit*, pp 4–12.

29 There is further discussion of these points in A Dunlop, 'Using the "Four Voices of Theology" in Group Theological Reflection,' *Practical Theology*, 14.4 (2021), 294–308.

30 G O'Neill and L Shercliff, *Straw for the Bricks: Theological Reflection in Practice* (London: SCM Press, 2018).

31 Ward, *op cit*, pp 39–53.

32 Ward, *op cit*, p 51.

33 Collins, *op cit*, pp 11–12.

34 Collins, *op cit*, pp 177–204.

35 See Collins' example of 'A ministry team with a problem,' *op cit*, pp 185–192.